PERMISSION TO PIVOT,

GRANTED

An Unapologetic Guide to Changing

Your Gotdamn Mind & Life

Kierra Asnuaskas

Copyright Page:

Permission to Pivot, Granted © Copyright <<2020>> Kierra Asnauskas

For more information, email kierra@missunconventional.com.

ISBN: 978-1-7364503-0-7

GET YOUR FREE AUDIOBOOK!

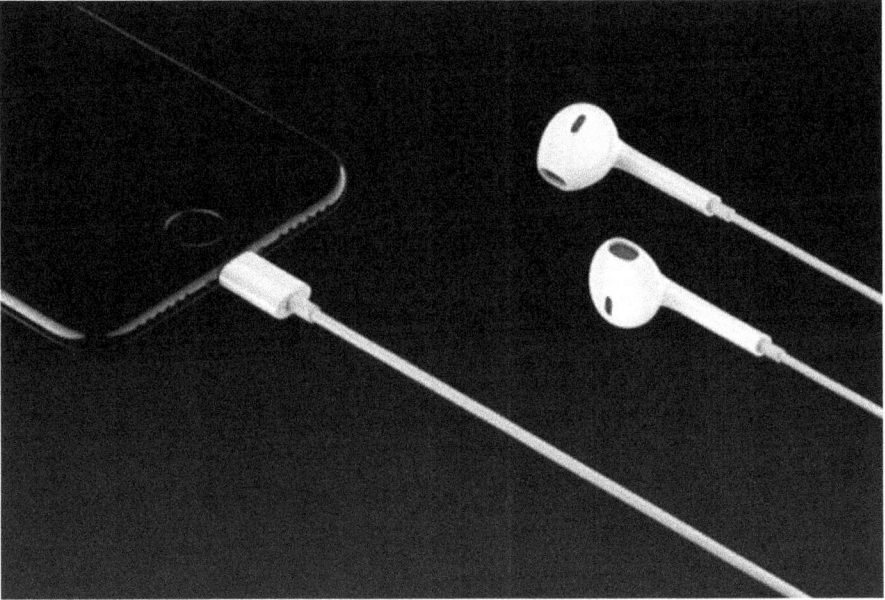

GET THE PIVOT PLAYBOOK!

To get the best experience with this book, I've found readers who invest in **The Pivot Playbook** are able to implement faster and take the next steps needed to make a purposeful, profitable pivot.

You can get a copy by visiting:
www.mypivotplaybook.com

Dedication

I dedicate this book to every woman out there struggling to grant herself permission to pivot in any area of her life. It can be hard and scary to decide to take charge of your life, but you've shown true courage just by picking up this book and being willing to take the first step.

TABLE OF CONTENTS:

Introduction:

D o you remember when you were little, and "playtime" often involved taking on the persona of someone or something else?

Maybe you played house, or put on plays, or even loved video games, and all of these activities required you to choose a character.

My own childhood obsession was playing the "Ready to Rumble Boxing" video game. There were multiple avatars to choose from, with catchy names like "Afro Thunder," "Big Willie Johnson," and "Selene Strike," but I always chose my girl "Lulu Valentine." For me, she represented sassiness, beauty, strength, fearlessness, and girl power! Although I resonated with her persona and could see myself embodying all those traits in the future, at the time I was NOTHING like that.

In fact, I had extremely low self-esteem. I would look in the mirror and beg God to lighten my skin. I hated the kink of my hair and despised the gaps in my teeth. Can you imagine feeling such a low self-worth at an age when all you should be thinking about is who's going to be "it" in the next game of hide-and-seek? It was heartbreaking, and I wouldn't wish that feeling on anyone.

I think deep down, that's why I'd choose Lulu Valentine as my avatar in the Ready to Rumble video game. She represented a look, physique, confidence, and fierceness I longed for. Not to mention, she could whoop a man's ass!

There was something powerful about that (although I of course do not condone violence towards men in real life).

Ahem. Moving on...

Little did I know at the time that real life is a lot like my old video game, in that we DO get to choose how we want to show up in life. Before we start the game, there's always a goal or agenda we must follow. Once we choose our avatar, we embark on a journey through the game to accomplish whatever our duty entails.

As we navigate the game, we are forced to make decisions. Those decisions lead to specific outcomes, which determine what we do next, and it goes on and on until we reach the end. Sometimes we find that reaching "the end" actually unlocks the door to another level of the game. On that level, the stakes are higher, the environment is different, and we are faced with new challenges.

If that's not the perfect metaphor for life, I don't know what is! In the game of life, you get to choose who you want to be, how you want to show up in the world, and what goals you wish to pursue. As you matriculate through life, circumstances inside and outside your control force you to make decisions about how you want to proceed.

Think about it. It's the same in video games, right? Monsters, adversaries, and villains come at you from every angle. You're ducking and dodging bullets, bombs, and beasts while trying to mastermind your next move. If you die in the game, it's game over... but not really, because you get to decide whether or not you want to go back in. When you do go back in, you simply pick up where you left off with the added knowledge about "what NOT to do." Real life is literally JUST LIKE THAT. When we live to fight another day, we approach that new day with a new perspective and list of lessons learned the hard way.

Choose Your Avatar

In the world of pivoting, there are two types of characters you can choose from: Stagnant Stacy and Audacious Audrey.

Stacy is stagnant because she rarely grants herself permission to pivot when it matters most.

- ✗ She'll stay in a career she hates because it's comfortable, easy, safe, and/or "respectable" in the eyes of her peers and family.

- ✗ She'll pursue a specific educational field out of obligation to her parents or because of how society views that particular field.

- ✗ She'll remain in an unhealthy relationship that no longer serves her due to comfort, familiarity, fear of being alone, or lack of confidence that she can find someone better.

On the other hand, there's Audrey, who lives her life audaciously because she always grants herself permission to pivot when the situation calls for it.

- ✓ If her career path is no longer serving her, she doesn't hesitate to re-evaluate and pursue a different path.

- ✓ If her field of study no longer supports what she needs to know for the mission she's on, she feels no obligation to "stick with it" for the sake of "sticking with it."

- ✓ The moment her relationships, platonic or intimate, stop serving her best interest, she's out like a thief in the night because she knows her worth, listens to her gut, and respects herself.

I was Stagnant Stacy once-- from 2011 to 2014, to be specific. I was pursuing a major I had lost interest in, but I felt married to it because I had already told people that's what I was going to do. I also didn't want to feel the shame of graduating later than my expected graduation year. It is easy to see in retrospect that the "shame" was a figment of my imagination, but there I was, thinking that people wouldn't respect me if it took me longer than the standard four years to graduate with my bachelor's degree.

I was ashamed of remaining in the food and beverage industry post-graduation because that's not what I went to school for, and I didn't want the time I spent pursuing that degree to be in vain (although no one actually said it would be). So I got the first "respectable" job I could find: Management Trainee at Enterprise Rent-A-Car. It wasn't even in my field of study, but it had the word "management" in the title, so it seemed like a "grown-up job" to me. Well, needless to say, that didn't last very long (not to mention, the whole thought process that led to that decision reeked of insecurity and baseless rationales).

After that failed, I reverted back to what I knew-- serving in the food and beverage industry. Why? Because it was safe, predictable, and comfortable (and I was flat foot broke!).

To top it all off, I was chasing a man who had all but spelled it out for me that HE DID NOT WANT ME. I chased and chased. I sacrificed my dignity with every plea, but he made it crystal clear that he was not willing to work it out. It was a relationship that should have ended in the first year it started, but I dragged it on (and off, and on again) for an extra four years because I thought he was the only man who'd ever accept me for who I was. I didn't think I'd ever be able to find anyone else like him. As toxic as the relationship was, I was addicted to the rollercoaster of it all. Little did I know, my desire for him was rooted in low self-worth.

Yup, I was Stagnant Stacy alright.

While this all may sound depressing, there is indeed a happy ending; as my girl Celie from *The Color Purple* said, "Trouble don't last always." but before we get to that happy ending, I have to ask:

Can you relate?

Or was I the only sista out here stagnant, stuck, and struggling? Asking for a friend...

Anyway, without further ado, with which avatar do you identify the most at this time in your life?

Check all that apply.

Stagnant Stacy:
☐ Lacks self-awareness
☐ Lacks clarity on her purpose and passions
☐ Seeks outside approval and validation before making decisions or setting goals
☐ Fears the uncertainty of paths and stepping outside of her comfort zone
☐ Feels paralyzed, unfulfilled, and dissatisfied with multiple aspects of her life
☐ Holds on to things, habits, goals, and people long after they've stopped serving her best interest

Audacious Audrey:

- ☐ Practices self-awareness daily

- ☐ Pursues her purpose and passions with urgency

- ☐ Seeks zero approval or outside validation for the decisions she makes regarding her lifestyle

- ☐ Embraces change, new adventures, and new opportunities

- ☐ Feels happy, fulfilled, and optimistic about the trajectory of her life

- ☐ Promptly abandons things, habits, goals, and people that no longer serve her best interest

I hope you identify with Audacious Audrey, but the unfortunate truth is that most people are more like Stagnant Stacy. Even if that's you right now, my goal is that by the end of this book you'll be motivated, inspired, and armed with the knowledge and the actionable steps to channel your inner Audacious Audrey. Why? Because it's her characteristics, mindset, and behavior that you'll need to embody in order to grant yourself permission to pivot and change your gotdamn mind!

The good news is, like a 90's video game, you get to CHOOSE who you want to be!

Can you guess who I chose?

Now we can get to the happy ending. In my case, after a few years of trial and error, I began to invest in courses, mastermind groups, and personal development books that helped me build the business and life I have today.

✓ I discovered my purpose, built a business around it, and gave myself permission to pivot any time the business model, products, or services no longer aligned with my mission or with the needs of my clients.

✓ I discovered my passions... the things that filled me up and brought me peace and happiness.

✓ I also found a man I didn't have to beg to love me. Whew! I never knew how powerful love can be when it's RECIPROCATED. I wish that kind of love for every woman out there.

In this game of life, there are roadblocks, surprise challenges, and setbacks that arise when we least expect it. These circumstances are not always within our control, but we CAN always control how we respond and which characteristics we'll embody to combat these challenges.

I've guided myself through a plethora of pivots (dozens, even!) by practicing self-awareness daily; pursuing my purpose and passions with urgency; seeking zero approval or outside validation for the decisions I make regarding my lifestyle; embracing change, new adventures, and new opportunities; feeling happy, fulfilled, and optimistic about the future; and promptly abandoning things, habits, goals, and people that no longer serve my best interest.

Don't get it twisted, though... I did not wake up like this. I worked hard to convert my Stagnant Stacy energy to Audacious Audrey energy. I had to take a long look in the mirror and decide whether I was going to let life happen to me, or if I was going to happen to life. It was a journey and a process.

Do you know what happened as a result of my decision to happen TO life?

I am now financially free, professionally fulfilled, happily married, and living my absolute best life.

I chose to embody the traits of Audacious Audrey every single time I was faced with a pivotal moment. I chose to listen to her voice at the start of each new season of my life. I changed my gotdamn mind more times than I can count... but there was a science to it.

I wasn't just changing my mind because the path became too difficult or because I just got bored. After analyzing how I navigated through a series of pivots in my life, I reverse-engineered the process and discovered that I was taking myself through what I now call the "The Pivot Protocol: Five Steps to Pivoting Like a Pro." I felt compelled to share this with the world, so that others could harness the life-changing magic of pivoting into their purpose. That is why you are reading this book.

Isn't that exciting?

What the Hell is a Pivot, Anyway?!

So, what the hell IS a pivot!? Inquiring minds want to know.

There are many ways to define a pivot, but in this book, we'll be discussing it as a shift, reversal, or change in our direction, decision, or goal that is due to one or more of the following:

- A drastic change in circumstances

- A drastic change in environment

- An influx of new information that is in direct contradiction to the old information

- A drastic decline in enthusiasm for a direction, decision, or goal because the end result no longer aligns with the season one is in

Pivoting is an analytical process, not an event. As we navigate the seasons of life, we encounter numerous forks in the road. The road we choose to take should always align with who we are and what will serve our best interests. Each road will either challenge us to level up or tempt us to remain the same.

So, when I speak of granting yourself permission to pivot, one or more of the above conditions need to apply.

This is not a book about changing your mind just because you don't feel like working hard anymore. Sorry. I will not be condoning quitting or giving up due to laziness or uncomfortable circumstances. So, if you're here hoping that I'll be making you feel better about breaking your promises to yourself and others for no good reason, you're going to be extremely disappointed.

If that's not why you picked up this book, thank God, because that would have been... awwkkwaarrdd...

Moving on...

What We'll Accomplish Together

Here is a list of my main goals for this book:

1. To adequately describe what the hell a pivot is--and why I feel qualified to teach it.

2. To teach you The Pivot Protocol, which is a 5-step process I've used throughout my journey to make drastic changes in my life.

3. To transparently reveal the potential pains of pivoting and major pivot pitfalls to avoid on your journey.

4. To describe what "pivoting like a pro" looks like in 10 different areas of life.

5. To highlight pro tips for pivoting and things to keep in mind as you open Pandora's box of possibilities when you choose to be Audacious Audrey.

Listen...

You get ONE life. Don't let someone else dictate how you live it!

Don't Be THAT Person

Don't be that person who skims through the book, and then claims the framework didn't work for you. Instead, be the kind of person who reads this book cover to cover, takes notes, answers the questions, and commits to taking action. Applied action is what ultimately yields results! That "go-getter" type is rare these days, but something tells me if you've read this far, you're that kind of person.

Intentions/Expectations

I wholeheartedly intend to deliver this message in a way that makes it life-changing, actionable, and inspiring for you. Allow this book to be your blueprint to making decisions FOR YOU, BY YOU. Many of us simply don't do that enough. I'm here to change the negative narrative around putting yourself first. It's time for our decisions, goals, and desires to take their rightful place in our lives: right up front, in the captain's seat.

I expect that you'll receive this message with an open mind and heart, ask yourself the hard questions, do the work needed to make a significant difference in your life, and take control of your destiny. Don't shy away from the discomfort of change; it's likely what you need to catapult you into your best lifestyle design. A little discomfort never killed anyone, last time I checked! And as my husband always says, "struggle builds character."

Let Me Lay It Out For You...

Allow me to make things easy for you with a snapshot of how this book is laid out.

First, we'll talk about the under-discussed and underrated, yet arguably most important, aspect of life: self-awareness. Beware, we're diving deep here. Trust me, you need this BEFORE we can discuss anything else.

After that, we'll cover the anatomy of a pivot, including a more detailed explanation, common myths and limiting beliefs. I leave no stone unturned, my friend.

Then, I'll reveal my "Pivot Protocol." This is what you came here for, and I plan to deliver the deets on a golden platter - forget silver!

What kind of book would this be if I didn't discuss the 10 most common types of pivots? Your girl is nothing, if not THOROUGH!

Finally, we'll delve into my strategies and pivot practices so you can walk away feeling unapologetic about granting yourself permission to pivot in whichever area of your life warrants it.

Ready?

Part 1

The Less Self-Aware, The More Painful the Pivot

Have you ever met someone who couldn't read a room? I'm talking about that person who's just oblivious to the mood and audience around them, and it's damn near painful to watch.

Or maybe, if we're being completely honest, we've been that person, but unfortunately didn't realize it before everyone was left with a not-so-great impression of us in that moment.

Self-awareness, folks. It's SO important, yet not sexy enough to get people's attention. It's not "newsworthy," controversial, or attention-grabbing enough to secure its place as a prominent self-help topic all on its own.

Nope, in fact, when personal development authors do write about it, they almost always have to cloak it in an awe-inspiring, catchy title because (let's be honest), who's going to pick up a book entitled, "The Importance of Self-Awareness"?

Very few would pick up that book.

With that said, it is my duty to explore this topic before addressing the world of pivoting. Why? Because without self-awareness, you'll become a victim to every pivot pitfall known to womankind... and we don't want or need that kind of stress in our lives. We have enough on our plates.

What is Self-Awareness, Really?

Most definitions you'll come across on "Google University" will describe self-awareness as "a conscious knowledge of one's emotions, desires, motives, and character." While this is correct, it leaves so much to be desired.

I define self-awareness as "a full 360-degree overview of how you take up space in the world." When you're aware of yourself, you have an understanding of how you come off to others, and you make peace with the fact that some people will love who you are, and some people won't. Let's be clear, just because you'll know how you come off to others, doesn't mean you have to care for everyone's opinion of you. For example, people used to tell me I was "too much," "too loud," or "not ladylike," and I would just brush it off with a.... "So?" (*shrugs shoulders*). I knew that was their perception, but as much as they were entitled to perceive me in that way, I was entitled to not give a damn. My mantra is, "I know I'm not for everyone, and I'm at peace with that."

There are layers to who I am. I'm multi-passionate, multi-talented, and complex. I don't fit into one box, and chances are, the same is true for you.

Self-awareness includes, but is not limited to, an analysis of one's:

- Strengths
- Weaknesses
- Values

- Talents
- Beliefs
- Motives
- Likes
- Dislikes
- Triggers (positive or negative)
- Personality
- Passions
- Purpose
- Other people's perceptions

All of these factors come together to make up the whole of who we are and how we show up in the world.

Why Should You Care About Self-Awareness?

Ignorance is NOT bliss in the case of cultivating self-awareness. What you don't know CAN actually hurt you, your relationships, your finances, and your progression at work or in business.

Sure, we know a thing or two after being in these bodies for so long, but have we really asked the hard questions regarding our weaknesses, triggers, motives, and purpose? I don't think so; and the data says "no," too. In fact, research shows that the majority of us sincerely believe we are self-aware, but only 10-15% of us actually are.

Imagine putting in blood, sweat, and tears to get promoted to a position at work, only to realize once you get it that the job magnifies your weaknesses and is not a position where your best self can shine.

Imagine chasing a love interest and finally capturing his or her heart, only to realize that every quirk they have is a serious trigger for you. I, for example, am an overly ambitious and goal-oriented person. Deep down, I know I cannot be happy long-term with someone who has no vision or big dreams for their life. You don't have to be Jeff Bezos ambitious, but you've got to give me something. Knowing this about myself, I can ask the right questions on dates (I'm happily married, but if I was still on the prowl...) and make sure I'm not setting myself up with someone I'll eventually outgrow.

Imagine being unaware of what motivates you, so you apply for a job that values and rewards external factors like sales and other output factors even though you're not a competitive person and you'd rather be recognized for your behind-the-scenes efforts like efficiency and customer satisfaction. Can you imagine how frustrating it would be for you to work in that competitive environment?

These are just a few examples, but hopefully you get the picture. Lack of self-awareness is a big deal. It's so much deeper than whether you're a vanilla or chocolate kind of girl. People who are highly self-aware don't need to pivot as much as people who aren't. They tend to be more productive, more confident, and unapologetic about who they are.

Have you ever met someone who constantly apologizes for existing? Women are especially guilty of over-apologizing, and a lot of that is rooted in lack of self-awareness. I'm writing this for me, really. If you feel convicted by this, that's your business. No judgment here.

I could write an entire book on self-awareness (and I probably will), but in an effort to stay on track, let's switch gears and discuss how the seasons of life relate to self-awareness and pivoting.

4 Distinct Seasons of Life:

When I speak of "seasons" here, I refer to what I like to call "The 4 Distinct Seasons of Life":

Season 1: The Copycat Season
Season 2: The Rebel Season
Season 3: The Q&A Season
Season 4: The Teacher Season

The Copycat Season:

This is the season most of us start out in. It describes that time in our life when we are almost unconsciously repeating what others say, doing what others do, and adopting the values, beliefs, and thoughts of those with whom we spend the most time.

As we grow older, we're supposed to grow out of this phase and begin to think independently. But I'm guessing as you're reading this, you can think of a person or two who's at least two or three decades into their life and still hasn't grown out of the "copycat" season.

Most children are in this season right now. They repeat everything their parents or friends say. They begin thinking the way they think, liking what they like, and believing all the things their parents believe with occasional moments of curiosity and rebellion.

Take my 8-year-old stepson, for example...

The first time I made grits for him, he didn't like them very much. However, over time, I was able to convince him that he liked them simply by talking about how amazing they were and getting his father to say the same thing. When I made them again six or seven months later, we reminded him how much he liked them the last time I made them. And of course, this time around, his face lit up and he said, "Oh wow, you're right! These are really good."

Let's set aside the possible ethical conundrum in my manipulation of an 8-year-old (we southern girls don't play when it comes to grits, ok?!) and focus on how I was able to get him to adopt my likes and beliefs around this food. It happens like this in so many areas of our lives.

Can you see how dangerous it could be to remain in this season of life as you grow older? As innocent as it is to manipulate children into eating their veggies or believing Santa Claus is real, the copycat effect can certainly be used against a person in this season

SN: Don't feel bad for my stepson. He's a master manipulator, always trying to get me to give him candy or soda, or take him to the Lego store, so I honestly don't feel bad. I've convinced him that he loves asparagus and water, too. We all use our powers in one way or another... I use mine for good!

The Rebel Season:

This is the season most people enter into during their adolescence. It describes that time in our lives where we're on a road of self-discovery. We're starting to experiment with abandoning the thoughts, beliefs, or actions that were bestowed upon us by a third party. We want to know what actually happens if we entertain those pubescent impulses that contradict what we've been told.

As we matriculate through this season, we learn lessons the hard way, discover what we're made of, what we like and dislike, what we stand for, how courageous we are, what we'll work hard for, etc. It's a process of self-discovery and awareness. Some of us take advantage of this stage and explore who we are, what we want, and how we want to live our lives, while others marinate in the dramas that arrive in this season.

Usually those between the ages of 16 to 25 or so (the actual age depends on many factors) experience this trial-and-error season. It's supposed to be fun, daring, and adventurous, but that's not always the case.

Take my little sister, for example:

She's 17 at the time of writing this book, and she's definitely in the "Rebel" season. She used to do every single thing we asked her to do; she would bring us the remote when we were too lazy to get it ourselves, repeat everything we'd say, and believe every little thing we told her, no matter how absurd. But now... it's a whole new ballgame. We can't tell her much of anything she doesn't consciously want to hear. She'll even research it to make sure it's factual!

In fact, more often than not, she does the exact opposite of what we tell her to do. She chooses when she wants to listen and when she doesn't. She'll take my advice on books to read or podcasts to listen to, but the moment I try to give my opinion about her joining the military, she shuts me down.

I can only smile to myself and say, "Good for her!" I teach people not to let the opinions of others dictate the decisions they make for themselves, and here I am trying to assert my opinion on my sister and she refuses to budge. That's what I'm talking about, Cherry! Tell me to go mind my own damn business, sis!

The Q&A Season:

This is the season most young and middle-aged adults are in, typically ages 25 through the early 40s. It describes that time in life when we start to question what career we want, whether we want to get married and/or have children (and if so, with whom?), where we want to live, etc. All of sudden, it feels like we, and the rest of the world, need "serious" answers to these questions. And heaven forbid our answers don't match the expectations of the mainstream.

As we navigate this season, we begin to zero in on our purpose (how we want to serve others) and our passions (how we want to serve ourselves), and if we're lucky, our previous season will have laid the groundwork for how we ultimately answer these questions.

On top of that, we'll have to get our finances in order, decide on a life partner (or not), and determine whether or not we'd like to bring children into the world.

Take me, for example:

This is the season I am currently in, and I'm probably a bona fide nightmare for a traditionally-minded person on the outside looking into my life. I am so unconventional it probably makes their stomach hurt.

I've decided to pursue the entrepreneurial path, I married outside my race to a man who does not share my views on God, I decided not to invest in a house in the U.S. at this time, I'm debt-free, I don't want to have any children (besides my stepson, of course), I invest my money in stocks and currencies rather than in retirement accounts like 401ks and Roth IRAs, and I fill my cup up and serve myself first, before assisting others. I'd say that I lead a very unconventional life, and I'm at peace with that.

The Teacher Season:

This is the season where most established people who answered many of the questions of the previous season reside. It describes the time in our life when we've "been there, done that" and now we're trying to pass on what we know to others.

Our entrance into this season is usually accompanied by a feeling of fulfillment and joy (assuming we've done right by ourselves in the previous seasons) and an undying desire to help others get to where we are. Being decent human beings, we'll want to teach everything we know to anyone willing to listen, and all of a sudden that part becomes what we wake up for every day... not to mention the opportunity to watch as your children (if you choose to have them) grow through the seasons and become who they're destined to be.

Most people who are approaching their 50s and beyond operate in this season, showing up in informal ways with their family members, colleagues, and friends, and in more official ways with strangers they mentor or coach.

Take Miss Lisa Nichols (Bestselling Author & Top Motivational Speaker), for example,

She found her purpose in inspiring people all around the world to be courageous and fierce in their pursuit of abundance and purpose. She's been doing it for a long time, and has stood on countless stages, spoken to millions of people in-person and virtually, written multiple books on personal achievement, and far surpassed her wildest dreams in terms of her lifestyle. Now, she feels it's her duty to teach others how to inspire, teach, and motivate the masses from the stage. She's teaching the craft that took her years to master. That's what it means to be in the "Teacher" Season.

Now that we have defined the seasons of life, the next step is learning how to cultivate self-awareness as we navigate the tragedies and triumphs that inevitably arise throughout these seasons.

The Six P's: Tools to Cultivate Self-Awareness

The cultivation of self-awareness can often be a subtle experience.

Maybe we travel to a new country, and we learn that we're more courageous than we thought or that we enjoy a certain style of travel over another.

Maybe we join a challenge and discover that we have a knack for motivating others or that we need constant accountability in order to achieve our goals.

Or maybe we notice that no matter where we are or who we make friends with, they always seem to use the same adjectives to describe us. It's subtle, but clear. Other aspects of self-awareness require deliberate analysis.

Personality:

Many of us have trouble responding to that totally general getting-to-know-you prompt: "So, tell me about yourself." We immediately start talking about the number of siblings we have, or our spouse, or even our professional background, but we struggle to just talk about the person we are.

Why is that? One could argue that we really don't know, on the conscious level, who we are and what sets us apart from others.

The truth is, personality has nothing to do with who your family is, what you do for a living, or where you live.

Personality is the characteristic set of our thoughts, feelings, and behaviors, which are mainly highlighted through our interactions with others.

Let's be real, it can feel weird and uncomfortable to answer "So, tell me about yourself" with a description of your thoughts, feelings, and behaviors-- especially if we have no idea what we think, how we feel, or how we act.

Here are some of my suggestions for cultivating self-awareness in terms of your personality...

The best and easiest way to start is by revisiting your journals if you have them. Then, the next lowest-hanging fruit is to take a series of free personality exams like the Myers-Briggs, Enneagram, and Core Values Index. After that, you can start asking close friends and family members how they would describe you.

Share your personality results with people who know you well and care about you, and ask them to highlight what they agree or disagree with based on their interactions with you. This can lead to powerful insights. So powerful, in fact, that when someone says, "So, tell me about yourself," you can respond with confidence.

Passions:

Some people view a passion as the thing they love to do and wish to earn money from, but this is not necessarily the case.

I define passions as the activities you do for your own personal joy, peace, and happiness. It's what you do to fill your cup, so to speak. Your innocent, selfish pursuits. It's what you do to reach peace, zen, and pure joy. It's how you serve YOURSELF.

Do you know why a lot of people are stressed and miserable? They keep trying to monetize their passion(s). Not only do they try to monetize it, but they associate their skill level, self-confidence, and self-worth with whether or not people will pay them for their passion.

This notion that "because I love to do this thing, I must make money from it" is the poisonous mindset that has squeezed the love out of what was supposed to be a passion project for many. This is not to say that we are never supposed to make money from our passions.

I talk about this in my book, "The Millennial's Unconventional Guide to Retiring Every Other Year: The Key to Designing the Life You Dream About."

But let's get a little more in-depth about how you can tell what your passions are, and whether or not you should try to make money from them.

The first step to determining your passions is asking yourself "What do I LOVE?"

Seem obvious? Bear with me here.

Asking yourself what brings you joy is the best way to identify your passions. I'll give you a few examples. I LOVE the following:

- Reading
- Traveling
- Dancing and singing to my favorite 90s R&B hits
- Trying new food at all kinds of restaurants
- Wine tasting

These are just a few of my passions. These activities bring me so much joy, and I do all of them FOR ME, no one else. I could technically monetize everything on this list, right?

- I could charge people to professionally review their books and articles.
- I could become a travel blogger and charge companies to travel on their behalf, capturing photos and videos and documenting experiences.
- I could join a cover band and get paid to perform other people's songs on cruise ships and resorts.
- I could become a food critic or food blogger and make money from sponsors.
- I could become a sommelier.

The thing is, I have no desire to do any of those things. I love these activities and monetizing them would take the love and freedom out of them. I don't wish to impact other people with these passions, and I don't consider others when I'm engaging in them either. I do them all for my own enjoyment, nothing else. Ask yourself what you love to do for YOU, and your answers are your passions.

Oftentimes, people confuse their passions with their purpose, which can cause issues like stress and anxiety.

Purpose:

The word "purpose" can feel like such a BIG word. It feels daunting because we think of it when we're assessing why we're here. Quite frankly, a lot of us don't know our purpose, and I think that has a lot to do with the fact that it has been inaccurately defined so many times.

If passions are how you serve yourself, then your purpose is what you do to bring joy, peace, and happiness to OTHERS. It's what you do to pour into the people around you, so to speak. Your innocent, selfless pursuits. It's what you do to show up and show out for other people.

Can you understand now how getting the two mixed up can make us stressed and miserable? A purpose can be monetized, but it doesn't have to be, either. It would make sense to monetize your purpose since it requires you trading your time and energy for the betterment and advancement of someone else, but even still, you have control.

If the first step to determining your passions is asking yourself "What do I LOVE?" then the first step to determining your purpose is asking yourself "What do I HATE?"

Seem like a weird question? Bear with me, because there's a method to the madness.

Ask yourself what you hate to see, what breaks your heart, what you wish wasn't so [as it relates to other people]. For me, this list includes:

- People not living up to their fullest potential and wasting the precious time they have
- People not setting themselves up for financial success
- People living their lives according to someone else's dream or vision
- People not investing in their personal and professional development
- People using fear of the unknown as an excuse not to act or follow-through on goals

I hated these things so much that I founded my company, Miss Unconventional, LLC, to combat them. It's a company that teaches entrepreneurs how to take control of their time, set intentional goals, and pursue their purpose with confidence and discernment without sacrificing their self-care. Some of the features of my business are not for profit, and some are. I get to decide. I write on my blog and post useful content on social media for free, but I offer one-on-one coaching, books, and digital products for profit.

In order for you to determine your purpose, you need to ask yourself what you hate to see in others, and if you hate it enough to be a part of the solution. If the answer is yes, you get to work on cultivating a solution. You commit to serving others who are doing or experiencing the thing you hate. Your "solution" should bring joy, peace, and happiness to their lives.

Peace:

Maybe you're thinking, "okay, what does peace have to do with self-awareness?"

Great question! I'm so happy you asked. My answer? A lot, actually.

If it's important to know your passions, purpose, strengths, weaknesses, emotions, etc., then it's also important to know what brings you peace and ease. Why? So you can deploy these practices or activities when things inevitably get tough throughout life and, more specifically, your pivoting process.

Think of peace as synonymous with self-care. Consider what you do to bring yourself back to center or to ease your mind. When you want to discover what brings you peace, ask yourself, "What brings me instant relief?"

It's possible you've never thought about this before, and that's okay. That's why I'm including it, because whatever you come up with will help you when you decide to "pivot like a pro" using my Pivot Protocol.

When I think of what brings me relief, I think of gratitude journaling, mindful meditation, and affirmations.

There is so much power in gratitude. Seriously, every time I think about throwing myself a pity party, I try to write down every single thing I'm grateful for and I INSTANTLY begin to feel better. I'd like to argue that practicing gratitude is the UNIVERSAL way to cultivate peace, but how you express that gratitude is wholly up to you.

Practicing mindful meditation has allowed me to clear my mind and visualize the best outcome for my life or specific situation. I release all the aspects of the situation I cannot control and take full responsibility and control over what I can, thereby making me feel powerful, hopeful, and secure.

I personally give my burdens to God and proceed with my life as if all is well. That's faith. My faith brings me peace. If you're not a spiritual person, what brings you peace may look different.

To determine what brings you peace, dedicate time to discovering which activities or practices provide you instant relief of worry or pain. When you discover it, practice it daily and watch your life transform before your eyes.

Past:

It is of utmost importance to be aware of your past, how you've previously shown up, and how any past trauma or tragedies are affecting your present and future.

Can one truly be self-aware without examining the effects of their past? I'd argue, no.

Analyzing the past can get tricky, though, and can sometimes lead to emotional paralysis. For this reason, I suggest some form of professional therapy to delve into any difficult or traumatic past experiences.

Even if you don't feel the need to hire a therapist, I do believe that thinking about how you grew up, the beliefs and values that were imprinted on you, and the environment in which you were raised can shed light on how you've come to be who you are, think what you think, and behave the way you behave today.

How did your parents view money? How were you treated when you made a mistake? Were you free to be yourself, or were your choices always dictated for you?

You need to analyze these questions in order to get an idea of how the answers may be affecting you now.

Don't be a victim to your past. Thrive in spite of it.

People:

The sixth "P" of cultivating self-awareness is, of course, people. We can't get the full 360-degree view of who we are without examining how we interact with others.

I'm talking about understanding how you come off to your parents, siblings, intimate partners, close friends, acquaintances, colleagues, bosses, and subordinates. Whew! It's a lot. For some people, just the thought of asking people to give constructive feedback is enough to make them want to vomit... especially because we know not all feedback will be praise. Listen, think of it as a challenge. Anything that's physically, emotionally, or mentally challenging builds character.

Here's the thing: you don't have to agree with everything everyone says about you, but you take back a little bit of power when you know exactly what they think and feel about you.

I'll give you an example:

Have you ever seen the movie "8-Mile" starring the rapper, Eminem? It's a movie based on what a white man's life was like growing up on the streets of Detroit as an aspiring rapper. He was broke, he was a product of a broken home, his mom was an addict, he was always on the verge of losing his job, and his girlfriend was unfaithful. But he was a great lyricist, and his closest friends knew it.

They encouraged him to enter rap battles with some of the best rappers in the city, but he usually choked from stage fright. The other rappers would harass and make fun of him and his lifestyle. They even beat him up one night.

Finally, he'd had enough. He mustered up the courage to go against each and every one of his enemies in a freestyle battle. When he reached his last and greatest opponent, he had to go first, which is usually considered a disadvantage.

Do you know what he did?

He began to rap about every single negative thing he knew the guy would say about him. He confirmed it all. He made fun of himself, and then he addressed the flaws in his opponent. Right before he dropped his mic, he said,

"Tell these people something they don't already know about me."

Can you imagine?

He completely undermined the other rapper's defense by disarming him with what he would have used against him. He knew all of his flaws. He embraced what was wrong with his life. He addressed every criticism everyone had about him. He was SELF-AWARE. Because he was self-aware, he was able to make peace with all of it in front of everyone and take a little power back.

I hope this story will help those who are afraid to hear what others have to say. It may hurt, but you will feel empowered by the knowledge. Not everything will be negative-- you may even realize that there are some positive ways you show up for people that you never previously gave yourself credit for.

Be fearless in your pursuit of their perspectives, because their perspectives are theirs, not yours, not everyone's, and certainly not objective reality. Remember that.

Self-Rediscovery: Who Were You Before You Were Told It Wasn't Okay?

When I interviewed my friend Michaela Paluck, life coach and host of the podcast "Live Aligned Radio," she told me that she always asks her clients,

"Who were you before you were told it wasn't okay?"

I got chills when she said this. I had a light-bulb moment when I realized that there was a time when we were able to be unapologetically ourselves. It probably didn't last that long for most of us, because adults have a way of shutting down any parts of our personality that make them uncomfortable, but there was a time.

I think about that time for me. I reflect on my pre-teen days, when everything that came out of my mouth naturally seemed like a shock and awe moment for the adults around me. For instance, there was the time when I was 8-years old, looking out the window in the back seat of the car, and I exclaimed,

"Oh, he is FINE!"

I was referring, obviously, to the handsome man we had just passed. My mom whipped her head around like I had just uttered a racial slur, or something similarly appalling. My young brain couldn't understand why it was wrong to comment that a man was cute. In my head, I was just stating facts.

Then there was the time my mom sat my sister and me down to give us the news that she was pregnant with my youngest sister, Cherish. I was 12 at the time. I had just learned about condoms in my health class at school. The teacher made it very clear: if you don't want to have a baby, you use a condom, and if you do want to have a baby, you don't use a condom.

My mom seemed nearly as confused and surprised by the news of her pregnancy as we were, and I didn't understand why. I asked her matter-of-factly,

"Well, did you use a condom?"

If looks could kill, I would have been dead. The woman was in complete and utter shock.

"Why would you ask me that, Kierra?!"

I explained to her that she sounded so surprised, but I had learned that if you don't want to have a baby, you use protection. Again, from my perspective, I was just stating facts and being my inquisitive self. I could see in her eyes that she wanted to whoop my ass; the only reason she didn't is because she didn't know what reason she'd give me for doing it!

I could name a million other instances like this, when my curious mind and outspoken nature were suppressed because they didn't fit my mother's definition of a "child's place" or because they "weren't ladylike." Don't ask questions in bible study, children should be seen and not heard. Don't fart, that's not how women should behave. Don't tell boys they're cute, they'll get the wrong idea. I would even hear adults around me worry that I'd end up a teenage single mom!

They were afraid because who I was seemed strange, uncomfortable, and foreign to them. I didn't fit their idea of what a child, or a woman, should be-- so I was told it wasn't okay.

So, there I was: sitting quietly, gassy and in pain from holding it in, stifling myself (and my flatulence) to please the adults around me. But look at me now: married, no kids, living my best life, and farting when I damn well please!

My point is, reflecting on who I was back then and who I am now has made me realize I didn't change a whole lot, but I can definitely see how others' words and reactions shaped who I am today. The criticism fueled me in a different way. I wanted to be unapologetically me, while proving them wrong and exceeding their expectations for my life.

Some people don't take it that way, though. Instead, they shrink and shrink and shrink until they are no longer the truest version of themselves. They no longer remember who they were before they allowed the opinions of others to dim their light. Because of this, they have to dive deep into the moments where they lost themselves and resurrect the person they once were and were always meant to be.

As life went on, I found that my moments of profound self-rediscovery happened when I was in new environments, surrounded by new people, with no one around to tell me to stop being me. The answer for you may lie in removing yourself from your current environment for a while if you've noticed that it doesn't allow you to freely express yourself.

That could look different for everyone. It could be a short trip somewhere, a long vacation, a permanent move to a new city, joining new groups, saying goodbye to old friends. Do whatever it takes, because no one should remain in an environment where they are forced to shrink.

Prerequisites for a Profitable Pivot

In addition to the six P's of self-awareness, I'd like to add this list of characteristics one should embody as they begin to grant themselves permission to pivot in each area of their life. Without the following, pivoting will be extremely painful.

☐   Growth Mindset

Those who have a growth mindset ask themselves "How can I learn to do that?" as opposed to clinging to the notion that they don't know or can't learn. A growth mindset is rooted in a strong belief that you have the ability to learn new skills with hard work and dedication. It's that "nothing is impossible" mentality.

☐   Thick skin

Those who have thick skin have an uncanny ability to restrain from getting angry or offended by other people's actions and words. Thick skin is rooted in your ability to receive criticism without succumbing to the urge to take it personally.

☐   Strong, compelling WHY

Those who have a strong, compelling "why" have a secret weapon when it comes to achieving their goals. On the road to success, the person who has a big "why" will be better equipped to withstand the struggles of the "how," because the "why" is strong enough to propel them forward. People who quit or give up easily are those who couldn't identify a "why" that was strong enough to weather the storms of the "how."

☐   Resilience

Those who are resilient are able to bounce back from difficult situations or conditions. They don't marinate in misery or sorrow. They allow themselves to be human and feel the pain of their conditions, but they don't use their unfortunate circumstances as an excuse to stay stagnant. They eventually pick themselves up and move forward.

☐ Independence

Those who are independent don't depend on others to get to where they want to go. Of course, these people understand that relationships are important and essential to success, but they don't rely on what other people do or don't do. They don't blame others for their negative circumstances. Their independence is rooted in their ability to take full responsibility for what they say, do, and feel.

☐ Open mind

Those who are open-minded are always willing to consider new ideas, possibilities, and paths. They know how to be objective, observant, and unbiased. Open-mindedness is rooted in your ability to respect and analyze all angles and perspectives of a situation but move forward intuitively towards the best avenue for you.

☐ Coachable spirit

Those who have a coachable spirit are able to ask for and receive feedback, and then take action on what they discover. Similar to having thick skin, having a coachable spirit means you can withstand criticism well, but when you're coachable you take the necessary steps to learn how to be and do better.

☐ All-in mentality

Those who have an all-in mentality are resourceful and creative. They play the hand they've been dealt and if it's not good enough, they play again. The all-in mentality is rooted in your ability to commit to doing the best you can with what you've got; and if what you've got is not much, then you have the tenacity to go out and get what you need.

☐   Patience

Those who have patience are able to maintain their composure even when things are not happening in their desired timeframe. Patience is rooted in your ability to be calm, cool, and collected when the universe decides not to give a damn about your timeline.

☐   Discernment

Those who have the gift of discernment are able to decipher and understand obscure or abstract situations. Discernment is rooted in your ability to envision the big picture even when some of the pieces of the puzzle are missing. It's right there alongside intuition and the ability to hear God's whisper.

Please don't fret if you don't check all these boxes. Chances are, as you embark on this journey and learn more about yourself and what it takes to design a great life, you will begin to cultivate these characteristics over time. I definitely didn't have all of these boxes checked when I began pivoting, but I noticed over time that as I cultivated each trait, each pivot became less painful.

Part 2
The Anatomy of a Pivot

Before 2020, how often did you hear or use the word "pivot?" Honestly, I didn't use it much. I unknowingly pivoted so many times, but I never labeled my actions as a "pivot." It was just me changing my gotdamn mind. Entrepreneurs were talking about adapting to the times, being forced to pivot, and they were mostly referring to business. But the truth is, for most of us, the year 2020 required pivots of epic proportions in more than just one area of life! Sure, career is important, but what about the other areas?

Earlier, I defined a "pivot" as "a shift, reversal, or change in our direction, decision, or goal that is due to one or more of the following:

- A drastic change in circumstances
- A drastic change in environment
- An influx of new information that is in direct contradiction to the old information
- A drastic decline in enthusiasm for a direction, decision, or goal because the end result no longer aligns with the season one is in"

I've been able to identify 10 major types of pivots:

1. Personal Pivots
2. Relationship Pivots
3. Professional Pivots
4. Educational Pivots
5. Spiritual Pivots
6. Lifestyle Pivots
7. Mental Pivots
8. Financial Pivots
9. Physical Pivots
10. Values-Based Pivots

As you were reading through that list, you may have thought about some pivots you've made in these areas just in the last year.

COVID-19 had us making relationship pivots when we realized our "quarantine bae" was actually intolerable; educational pivots because schools shut down; spiritual pivots because people start praying a whole heck of a lot more in the midst of a pandemic; lifestyle pivots because shrimp dinners and Spanish wine had to be replaced with instant ramen and tap water; financial pivots because we had to "rob Peter to pay Paul;" physical pivots because we had to become disciplined enough to exercise at home rather than at the gym; and professional pivots because many of us could no longer go into our workplace. I mean, I could go on and on. The pivots of 2020 were endless. It all happened so fast and all at once, that we forgot we've actually been pivoting in these areas for years. It's just different when it's done under the pressure of a global pandemic.

Here's a brief description of each type of pivot:

Personal Pivots

You've experienced this type of pivot before, right? It's when you say to yourself at the end or beginning of every year "I'm going to get my entire life together this year, watch!" You begin establishing morning routines, developing new habits, tapping into your adventurous side... all the things.

These types of pivots usually happen around a new year, new quarter, or around our birthdays. These are times when we're reminded that striving to be the best version of ourselves is a great idea and we should try again even though our previous attempt failed.

In a nutshell, personal pivots deal with changes or shifts in routines, habits, hobbies, and passions. They tend to be difficult to execute, because they require a shift in day-to-day behavior and mindset. If you have the kind of personality where you can quit habits cold turkey and adopt new ones, you may thrive; but few of us are naturally this way, so personal pivots often require accountability and frequent motivation in order to "stick with it."

Relationship Pivots

If you go through life without experiencing a few relationship pivots, are you even human? I'm talking intimate, platonic, familial, and professional relationship pivots. By the end of the Rebel Season, you will likely have experienced at least half a dozen pivots in this area.

Think about your relationships in the last 3–5 years. How many of them have stood the test of time? Out of those, how have the dynamics of those relationships changed?

I'll give you an example. A friend of mine was in a relationship with a man that treated her like a queen in the beginning, but at some point, that treatment began to wither away. He became distant, they stopped having meaningful conversations, they began to argue about everything, and eventually they just couldn't stand being around each other. She had a choice: stay or go. She chose to go. Why? Because the relationship was no longer serving her best interest, or his.

Sometimes, we treat seasonal people like forever people and forever people like seasonal people. This is a major pivot type because when emotions get involved, they can cloud our judgment, and we end up learning lessons the hard way in this area of life. If you don't use the Pivot Protocol for any other area, use it for this one. It may save you from unnecessary heartbreak.

Professional Pivots

This is the most commonly discussed, analyzed, and written about type of pivot. Unless you are one of the rare exceptions, you WILL have to make multiple professional pivots in your life. We have all heard those stories about how, "back in the day," you worked for one company for 30 to 40 years, retired, and received a gold watch. That's great and all, but how many stories have you heard like this in the 21st century? Not many. Attitudes are set up differently nowadays, and most people can hardly stand the same spouse and child for 20 years, let alone a corporate job! Amiright?

Think about the jobs, careers, and side hustles you've held in the last 3-5 years. If you haven't changed companies, think about promotions you've had or new roles you've taken on. Any change or shift dealing with how you make a living is considered a professional pivot.

Take me, for example. I thought I was going to stay in the TESOL field for at least five years, but when I was teaching in Afghanistan, I had a strong urge to pursue a degree in human resources. I thought I would be on track to land a spot in a well-respected Leadership Development Program. I had no idea that in the midst of that pursuit, God would reveal to me my true calling: to teach young entrepreneurs how to design the life and business of their dreams. I couldn't understand why I didn't even get interviews for HR positions that I was more than qualified for, until I realized those rejections were redirections. All of the professional pivots led me to my purpose, and for that I am grateful.

Educational Pivots

We've all seen it, right? We've seen people change their mind and drop out of school, switch their major last minute, or decide to forego formal education altogether and dive straight into the workforce.

The problem is, unless you're Mark Zuckerberg or Bill Gates, no one commends you for dropping out. Unless you're Michael Jordan or Beyonce, no one praises you for foregoing formal education altogether. And unless you're switching from liberal arts to STEM, no one applauds your decision to switch majors.

We're constantly bombarded with everyone else's perfect view of what education should look like. It looks something like this: finish high school, go to college, study something that makes other people think you're smart or will lead to a high-paying job, blah, blah, blah. But did anyone stop to think that it makes zero sense to push this narrative of the perfect educational sequence on everyone without regard to, well, anything!? I can think of a bazillion reasons why it's problematic, but that would require me to go far beyond the scope of this book.

But here's one simple reason: Not everyone needs a "formal" education to do what they want to do!

If someone wants to start a travel blog and make money as an affiliate marketer or get paid for their videos or photos, why on Earth would that person need to go to a four-year university first? She could take online courses, hire a private photography coach, or pay for videography lessons, but a formal education would not necessarily make or break this person's career aspirations.

Those of you who are thinking:

"Well, what if she changes her mind and wants to do something that DOES require formal schooling?"

To that I say, "Good for her! She changed her gotdamn mind, now she needs to go do what she has to do to reach her goal."

Plain and simple.

But can you imagine going into thousands and thousands of dollars' worth of unnecessary, unforgivable debt when what you wanted to do didn't even call for it? I'm triggered just writing this. I thank God for my education, and I don't regret it because at the time, I did want to do something that requires a formal degree. But that's not always the case.

Spiritual Pivots

Most people don't consider spiritual pivots because they seem to happen infrequently compared to the other types of pivots, but it's important to highlight them here.

Spiritual pivots are associated with your religious beliefs, plain and simple. The reason why pivots don't happen nearly as often in this area is because we're dealing with fundamental beliefs and values that are normally passed down from our parents when we were in that Copycat season I mentioned earlier. Most people stick with whatever they were raised to believe about a higher power and how the world came into existence. Beyond that, spiritual practices like prayer, going to a place of worship etc. all fall under this category.

I've made a couple spiritual pivots in my life. The first was when I was younger and my mom, along with one of the pastors and a few members of the church, no longer liked what they were witnessing in the church we went to. Instead of abandoning church altogether, my pastor decided to host those who decided to leave at his apartment. It was about 10-15 of us.

We began having "church" every Sunday at his apartment. It was great while it lasted, and definitely a drastic shift for us. I was old enough when this happened that I made my own decision to attend and participate.

There are more extreme pivots in this area, like when someone converts altogether to a different religion or when a believer becomes an atheist. This type of pivot does happen more frequently than we think.

Lifestyle Pivots

Did you ever get a significant raise or a new job that pays more, and the first urge you felt was to "level up" your lifestyle by buying new car or clothes or even moving into a nicer place? That's a lifestyle pivot.

This type of pivot deals mostly with the material characteristics of your life, as well as the quality of your experiences. Think about where you live, the food you eat, the car you drive, the places you travel to, your means of travel, and the types of social engagements you attend.

Any change or shift dealing with the things that make up your "social status" is considered a lifestyle pivot.

For example, I used to be a budget traveler. I enjoyed staying in hostels and couch surfing because it was cheap, and I got to meet amazing new friends. I ate street food or cooked all my meals. I took buses and trains as opposed to a plane whenever possible and when I did choose to fly, I always flew economy. Then, I began to make more and more money. I got older and began fancying the finer things in life. My tastes changed and while I still love to travel, I no longer want or need to travel on a strict budget.

Mental Pivots

Now, this type of pivot may be the hardest of them all. Why? Because the greatest battles are usually fought within our own minds. It takes conditioning and reprogramming to pivot mentally.

Mental pivots deal with mindset shifts and ways of thinking. Think about the mindset you have regarding topics such as education, race, love, and money. Any change or shift dealing with your thought processes and perception of the world around you is considered a mental pivot.

The biggest mental shift I've ever made was my mentality around what's possible for a young black woman in business for herself. I don't think I realized that black women can be 6- and 7-figure solopreneurs. I knew we could have small businesses, but I think on a subconscious level I wasn't convinced that we could build 7-figure coaching businesses like the Tony Robbinses and Brendon Burchards of the world. It was only when I started surrounding myself with the type of women who shattered that limited thinking with the way they showed up in life and business that I began to believe that we are just as capable, and it is being done by women who look just like me. These women have receipts! I was empowered and inspired, and now I know that I can do it too. My mentality has completely shifted.

Financial Pivots

If you're thinking this type of pivot is the same as lifestyle pivots, think again.

While lifestyle pivots can sometimes have money-related motivations, financial pivots deal directly with the way you handle money.

For example, I used to believe in the power of social security, retirement accounts, and pensions, but the experiences in my life have led me to take more control over my finances by learning how to manage my own accounts and not relying on government programs to be my only saving grace when I "retire."

As a result, I'm learning how to day trade, manage my own investment portfolios, and seek other ways to make, save, and invest my money.

I used to think that debt, especially student loan debt, was just a part of life; it was just something we all have and would always have. But I realized that becoming debt-free was synonymous with freedom, and I decided to pay off all of my debt and invest my money in stocks, currencies, and my brain of course!

Financial pivots can be tough, but I find that those who make the best financial decisions are those who spend time educating themselves on the subject. I've read dozens of personal finance books, and I've taken a little bit of power back with each book I read.

Physical Pivots

Have you ever gone from skinny to fat, then fat to skinny, and back again? No? Ok, so… just me then? Sometimes, I feel women have just been hardwired to feel like we all have to change our bodies in some way or another.

Physical pivots deal with health and fitness-related decisions. Workout regimens, eating habits, internal health treatments and supplements, and preventative care practices are all under this umbrella.

Any change or shift dealing with the way you treat your body is considered a physical pivot.

I recently made the decision to change my diet and exercise regimen under the supervision of a personal trainer, and it was the best decision I ever made. I gave up carbs, sweets, dairy, and overeating. At the end of 90 days, I was 8lbs. lighter, healthier, more energetic, and confident. My mission to improve my health is one example of a fairly common, yet powerful, physical pivot.

Values-Based Pivots

One might assume this type of pivot is like spiritual pivots, in that our values don't change as frequently, but we do have to pivot in this area more often than we think. For instance, when you were in your Copycat Season, did you really value things like time and financial freedom? Probably not. As we grow, evolve, and matriculate through the seasons of life, certain values like family, integrity, stability, and independence may become more or less important to us.

When I was young, single, well-paid, and active, some of my values included travel, social relationships, and physical fitness. After I got married, my values shifted to family, financial security, and time management. This is not to say that values are exclusive to specific lifestyles, it just means that when your lifestyle changes, the things that are important to you or take priority in your life will inevitably change with it.

Now you know the ten types of pivots, and I bet you can identify a time when you've had to pivot in one or more of these areas, but the main question I always get is,

"How do I know if it's time to pivot?"

So, let's dive deeper into the questions you need to answer before deciding to pivot.

The Six W's: Pivot with Purpose

The W's of a Pivot are made up of six questions:

1. Which area of life warrants a pivot?

Rate each area of your life on a scale of 1 to 5, 1 being "needs improvement" and 5 being "highly satisfied." Pay close attention to the areas you give a rating of 1–3. This is your starting point.

2. Who should determine if a pivot is warranted?

Once you've identified the area(s) that need improvement, you want to list the people involved in this area of life. If you will be the only one affected, then there's no need to write this list.

3. Why should you pivot?

Next, you want to write down all the reasons why you think you should pivot in this area(s). List the pros and cons.

4. When should you pivot?

After listing the pros and cons and analyzing the "why," you'll have a better idea of how severe the situation is. The severity of the issue will help you determine when you need to initiate the pivot. There is no barometer for this. Only you can say what's tolerable or intolerable. My advice is: if the pain of staying the same outweighs the potential pains of change, then it's time.

5. What should you do to prepare for a pivot?

Once you've made the decision to pivot, you need to figure out how you're going to navigate the pivot. Who needs to know? Does it require any physical or environmental changes? Which actions do I need to take to make the transition as smooth as possible? Do I need a Pivot Partner?

6. How many times have you pivoted in this area?

The only reason I include this question is because you want to make sure there are no unhealthy patterns here. There is no set number of times for pivoting in any area of life. You decide. BUT if you find yourself always having to pivot in a particular area of life, you may need to take a step back and determine if there's a deeper issue.

Are your gears turning?

You've been here before, right? You've been in that place where you've had to decide whether or not to stay the course when it came to a particular field of study, a job, or a friend or partner. We all have to deal with these decisions. The truth is, many of us make our decisions or set goals within these areas based purely on emotion-- and that's where we miss the mark.

Decisions in these areas require attention to detail, logic, and analysis. Does that sound too "business-y" for you? It's supposed to. People believe that "strategy" is just a term for business, but it's not. It applies to life as well, and when you create a strategy for your life, you set yourself up for success. Let me give you a few examples of the difference...

Education: You begin college with the intention to study law, but the classes prove to be much harder than you anticipated. You meet someone who dropped out of law school, but still became successful, so you think to yourself,

"Well, if I drop out, I can still be successful like this person. So, I'm just going to quit, because I'm failing anyway."

No deep introspection.

No analysis.

No pros v. cons evaluation.

Just a weak rationalization for quitting because the path was harder than anticipated.

Career: You make the decision to go full-time as an entrepreneur. You come up with what you feel is the perfect product or service, you spend months and thousands of dollars on development and bringing the product or service to market, and when it launches... CRICKETS. You immediately feel discouraged and determine that the failure of the launch means no one's interested in what you have to offer, and this isn't for you. You close up shop.

No deep introspection.

No analysis.

No research to determine the cause.

Just a weak rationalization for why it didn't work out and why it never will.

Relationship: You've been friends with this girl since childhood. You two had every class together, studied together after school, and even snuck out to parties together. But as you've matured, the friendship has changed. It feels one-sided. You seem to be progressing and happy in life, but your friend seems to be stuck. Every conversation is about her, and you stopped benefiting from the relationship a long time ago. Still, you stay in the friendship because it's familiar and lots of time has been invested.

Again...

No deep introspection.

No analysis.

No real talk session.

Just a weak rationalization for staying in a friendship that stopped serving your best interest years ago.

Do you see what I'm trying to point out here?

Oftentimes, we make decisions based on our "feelings" or the feelings of others and it leads us down a path that doesn't serve our highest self, and then we wonder why we are unhappy and unfulfilled. We feel like we can't afford to change our mind, do things differently, or choose a new path because the fear of loss creeps in. The reality is, we often fear losing something or someone we were never meant to hold onto in the first place.

And herein lies the need for strategic analysis in our life. We start by asking and answering the six W's to get to the root of whether or not a pivot is warranted. Asking ourselves and being honest with ourselves about the which, who, what, when, why, how of a situation is how we start to make sound decisions about the most important aspects of our lives.

And at the root of all of this is selfishness and self-preservation. Because the truth is:

- A mother can be of no real value to her children if she's neglected herself and her best interests.

- A teacher can be of no great value to her students if she does not take care of herself first.

- A boss can be of no great value to her employees if she neglects to fill up her own cup.

- A wife can be of no great value to her husband if she neglects to address the true desires of her heart.

- A student can be of no great value to herself if she has yet to come to terms with how and why she learns.

- A person can be of no great value to the world if she has not laid the foundation and done the hard work to reach her highest self.

You get the picture. My point is, it's time to start making decisions and setting goals for our lives based on something more meaningful than emotions. It's time to start making decisions that align with our personality, our purpose, our passions, and the season that we're in. It's time to start making our mind align with our gut. It's time to begin pursuing what's right for us, no matter what other people think or how they may feel. A life well-lived should be a life that is a perfect representation of a pursuit to reach our highest self.

If right now you're feeling like I have a point, but you're not sold, keep reading...

Part 3
The 5-Step Pivot Protocol

C an I ask you something?

Do you think you can take a woman seriously who has changed her gotdamn mind dozens of times?

Do you trust that I have the juice on the proper way to pivot?

I mean, if you've read this far, then your gut is probably telling you to trust me. And your gut would be right, if I do say so myself.

I've pivoted more than your average 29-year-old, and to some, that fact is not cute, admirable, or worthy of praise. It may seem like I'm unable to commit or stay the course, or like I give up far more often than I stick with it.

But those of you who know that experience is the greatest teacher, know that's not the case.

My plethora of pivots are exactly what gives me "street cred."

You see, I was never meant to lead an ordinary life. I've literally been marching to the beat of my own drum since I was 10 months old and decided to walk my little ass right out the house and down 24 brick stairs! Thanks, Uncle, for leaving the door open!

By the grace of God, I emerged from that incident with just a bump on my forehead and a frantic and distressed mother. The point is, I chose a path, pursued it, stumbled, got bruised, and hurt some feelings along the way, but I was FINE. I didn't die.

So basically, I've been approaching life like that since then, but mitigating risks a little better. And when I came to the realization that my number one duty was to myself since I only get one life, all bets were off and I began doing me, unapologetically. A plethora of pivots later, I'm writing this book and coaching ambitious, goal-oriented, professional women on goal setting, productivity, vision boarding, and lifestyle design. I'm married to an amazing man, encouraging him to pursue his dreams with a fierce urgency, and I'm surrounded by the most positive, goal-oriented, audacious boss babe friends a girl could ever ask for.

Like Rascal Flatts said, "God blessed the broken road that led me straight to you."

I learned far more about myself than I would have if I'd never taken any bold risks. I learned that I love to travel, I love languages, I love spicy Thai food. I learned that I love Croatian rakija and La Rioja Spanish wine. I learned that I could survive and thrive in an environment where I'm the only foreigner and no one speaks my language. I learned that I could love and respect people from various backgrounds who have different beliefs and values.

Could I have learned all of this about myself had I never granted myself permission to pivot? I seriously doubt it.

I've gone through major pivots in my education, career, and relationships and all of those pivots still led to the path I was destined to be on from the beginning.

Take my education & career pivots, for example:

I thought I was going to major in Pharmacy and attend Duquesne University. Well, as I matriculated through high school, I realized I sucked at chemistry and calculus, and I knew I did not have the nerves to deal with the pressure of making sure medication orders were accurate. I couldn't imagine ever being responsible for someone's health like that, no matter how much money I'd make.

#PERMISSIONTOPIVOTGRANTED

Next, I began to think I might have a shot at becoming a U.S. Diplomat. After all, I loved AP U.S. Government & Politics, loved studying other cultures, and absolutely loved flaunting my Spanish skills, so I decided to major in International Relations. Then Benghazi happened. Let's just say that situation was enough to make me reconsider how dedicated I was to devoting my life to the international advancement of my country's political agenda. No thanks.

#PERMISSIONTOPIVOTGRANTED

So, there I was, feeling depressed and lost because I was no longer going to pursue a career in the field I just spent four years learning! I decided to pursue a TESOL (Teach English to Speakers of Other Languages) certificate before embarking on my journey to teach English in South Korea. I thought it would be the beginning of a long journey teaching English to kids across various countries, but then I realized my sassy attitude and sarcasm was not appropriate for educating people's children. Plus, my motto, as I dealt with more and more rascals, became "If I can't beat your kid, I can't teach your kid."

But wait, I thought, just because my personality is not right for teaching kids, doesn't mean it's not right for teaching adults! So I jumped at an opportunity to teach English to women who served in the Afghan National Army and Air Force in Afghanistan. While I enjoyed that much more, I was enraged by the incompetence of the Human Resources department for the company I worked for at the time, and thought to myself, you know what, "Instead of being mad, I'm going to go study for my MBA in Human Resources Management in Zagreb, Croatia and show these people what a competent human resources professional is supposed to look like."

#PERMISSIONTOPIVOTGRANTED

For a moment, I thought I may have a place in the corporate world as a Human Resources professional. When I saw how horrible the HR representatives at my previous company were, I thought, "You know what, let me get into this field and show them how it's done!" As I studied, I began pursuing a side hustle geared towards personal development, goal setting, and vision boarding. One business retreat in Malta was enough to get me to abandon my MBA ambitions and pursue my business, Miss Unconventional, full-time!

#PERMISSIONTOPIVOTGRANTED

All of those pivots, many in between, and many after led me to what I pursue now. Entrepreneurship, individual achievement, marketing, course and curriculum design, event planning, non-fiction writing, and public speaking are the kinds of topics I study now. I continue to educate myself according to the knowledge I need to reach the next level.

My purpose. My calling. My reason! As a Lifestyle Design Strategist, Author, Speaker, and Founder of Miss Unconventional, LLC, I have reached alignment with my personality, purpose, and passions. The experiences I had before this were there to prime and mold me.

Take my relationship pivots, for example:

I thought the first guy I dated seriously was a real keeper. He treated me like a queen, he treated my mom like a queen, and his love language was "Acts of Service" so he was always going above and beyond. My younger self believed he could be the one, but one day I was invited to his house and I saw a different side to him.

His mom was so accommodating, especially considering our age. She offered to make us food and she was really hospitable, but that boyfriend, who shall remain nameless, yelled at her to leave us alone and that we didn't need anything. When she backed away sad, feelings hurt, I knew from then on, the way a man treated his mother would be a major factor in whether I dated him or not.

#PERMISSIONTOPIVOTGRANTED

Then there was my college sweetheart. I REALLY thought he was the one, but it never made sense. We were constantly on again and then off again, our relationship plagued with infidelity and lack of trust, and the arguments were toxic and unhealthy. I think I cried more days than I smiled. My self-esteem was low and my confidence non-existent. At some point I got sick and tired of begging to be loved and that was that.

#PERMISSIONTOPIVOTGRANTED

It was about two and a half years before I dated again. The next relationship was driven by lust more than anything and when I decided to pursue a new career path, he had no interest in following me, so we ended amicably because our paths were no longer aligned.

#PERMISSIONTOPIVOTGRANTED

Then I met the man who is now my beloved husband. He was kind, chivalrous, strong, confident, and perhaps most importantly, completely and irrevocably in love with me. He treated his mother like a queen, loved and cared for his son and family, was fiscally responsible, respected my beliefs and ambitions, and accepted me flaws and all. He was the one that made me enthusiastically abandon the single life forever, and I couldn't be happier.

All of this to say, your girl knows a thing or two about pivoting. As random as some of those pivots may seem, they were indeed well thought out, analyzed, and assessed for risks vs. reward and pros vs. cons. It doesn't take me long to make a decision, but I do my due diligence. Once I commit to the decision, that's it. I own it. I make a plan and then work that plan while giving myself time to adjust.

At the time of writing this book I am 29, and when people hear my story plus my age, they gasp in disbelief because to them it seems I've lived five different lives. And in some ways, I have. I've traveled to almost 30 countries, lived and worked in three, learned a new language, made friends from all different cultures and backgrounds, hosted events and workshops, managed teams, and achieved financial freedom. But I started broke, with 89 cents to my name, severely depressed and suicidal. My car was repossessed, my credit cards maxed out, and I was $50,000 deep in student loan debt.

That was my foundation. I am the product of an African American single mother household with three younger sisters. My mother had me when she was 17 years old. My father wasn't always present throughout my childhood and adolescence. The first nine years of my life were spent living in the ghetto of North Memphis. Statistically speaking, I'm an anomaly. No way on God's green Earth should I have made it this far, but by the grace of God, I am here.

When you have the mindset that "it can only get better from here" and when you feel that in your bones, it usually does. I want you to win. I need you to win. I need you to experience what it feels like to be in control of your every move.

I'll be honest, I didn't realize there was a method to my madness before I decided to reverse-engineer how I successfully pivoted when the situation warranted it. I hadn't given it much thought until I was constantly being asked how I conjured up the courage to take certain leaps, I had no eloquent way to put it. I thought, "Oh, you know, I just did it." But the truth is, my process was much more strategic than that. I've always been a strategic thinker, and my mind assesses situations a lot more quickly than most. I love efficiency and decisiveness. I value time, and I make decisions quickly and efficiently.

When I reverse-engineered my thought process and actions for each major pivot in my life (including the ones I shared above), I realized it all boiled down to the six W's above and these five main steps...

Step 1: Determine If & When a Pivot Is Warranted

This step is number one for a reason. It requires deep introspection and self-awareness. It's that one thing that keeps you from making a decision or setting a goal purely off of emotion. As I began to travel, test my limits, and do challenging things, I learned more and more about myself. This self-awareness allowed me to ask the hard questions and be real with myself.

I'd ask questions like:

"Kierra, how is this situation serving you right now?"

"Kierra, what's your end goal here?"

"Kierra, is staying in this situation worth it? If so, why?"

"Kierra, are you just quitting because shit is hard, or do you actually have a valid reason to switch gears? If so, what are those 'valid' reasons?"

"Kierra, does this situation/goal/experience bring you joy?"

"Kierra, are you sick and tired of being sick and tired? If so, why?"

"Kierra, if you make this decision now, what's the worst-case scenario?"

"Kierra, if you make this decision now, what's the best-case scenario?"

"Kierra, if you wait longer to make this decision, what's the worst-case scenario?"

"Kierra, if you wait longer to make this decision, what's the best-case scenario?"

"Kierra, is the pain and discomfort you feel right now great enough to deal with consequences of the worst-case scenario?"

"Kierra, what would Grandma tell you to do? She always wanted you to choose the most authentic path. What would she say?"

When you can ask yourself the hard questions, play the devil's advocate, assess the situation, and determine your real motives, you can trust yourself to make sound decisions. It would be easy to read a title like "Permission to Pivot, Granted: An Unapologetic Guide to Changing Your Gotdamn Mind & Life" and think that I was just out here quitting when things got rough and making excuses for changing my goals and direction, but that's not how I operate.

All of these questions crossed my mind, and I made sure I answered them every time. I'm no quitter. Am I a habitual experimenter? Sure! But a quitter, no. I simply give myself permission to stop doing things that don't serve me, and I teach others to do the same.

I remember when I was faced with a decision to renew my contract on the cruise ship or pursue a new career in teaching English abroad in South Korea.

I was real with myself the whole time. Is this the right time to leave? Is this place serving my best interest at the highest level? What will I gain by staying? What will I gain by leaving? What's the worst-case scenario if I leave now? Am I afraid to leave because I'm comfortable? Am I showing up as my best self on this ship? Is this position bringing me joy? What are the pros and cons to leaving?

Yes, I asked and answered all of those questions as I was preparing to embark on this new endeavor of teaching English abroad. The results were in, and it was time to go. The analysis was complete. It was, indeed, the time to grant myself permission to pivot.

I had originally planned to stay working on the cruise ship until I paid off all of my credit card debt, which at the time was a little over $12,000, but the new opportunity would allow me to save more while experiencing a higher quality of life, so I changed my gotdamn mind!

Which brings me to step number two...

Step 2: Plan Your Pivot Like a Pro

I mean, think about it. What's the use in doing all that deliberating and risk analysis and not formulating a solid plan after the decision has been made, right? Plus, this is just how I love to do things. I write shit down, prepare to-do lists, map out the steps it'll take to get to where I want to go in the most linear way possible. That's how my brain works. I go into research mode, sometimes traveling down a deep rabbit hole of all the ways I can achieve this next goal.

I do things like:

- ✓ Find people who are where I want to be and ask for guidance.

- ✓ Read blogs and books on best advice and practices.

- ✓ Research requirements or anything I need to have in place in order to make my transition as smooth as possible.

- ✓ Research the pros and cons of what I was planning to do from other people's perspectives and determine if their gripes would be something that would trigger me based on my personality and overall goals.

Yes, people, it gets that real in the planning phase. I remember as I was preparing to make the transition from working on the cruise ship to teaching in South Korea with EPIK, I kept reading about how the process was "so long" and you probably won't hear back for two to three months. I literally interviewed for the position on a Tuesday and was told I was accepted by Friday!

How did that happen? I told myself I would not start the application process until I had all my ducks in a row. I reviewed the requirements on the application, added those documents to my to-do list, and went to work. I started a TESOL Certification program, wrote my statement of purpose, paid extra to have my federal background check notarized and apostilled expeditiously, gathered three letters of recommendation, and researched common interview questions that I found on blogs. I didn't reach out to a recruiter until I had a folder on my desktop with scanned copies of all the documents aforementioned and I was one month away from passing my certification course.

When I finally reached out, I was able to send the recruiter (who I thoroughly researched prior) an email with all the required documents (with some information redacted) before he even asked. This was my way of letting him know I meant business. I told him I was open to teaching anywhere BUT Seoul, something he had probably seldom heard. I made his life easy because I came prepared.

There's a dichotomy here that a lot of people can't handle: having a plan in place for a strategic pivot, yet not allowing oneself to get too attached to the "HOW." Basically, I always had a plan, but if the process didn't go exactly as planned, I wouldn't get bent out of shape about it. I would pivot within the pivot.

It boils down to being prepared, but not getting sucked in by over-planning the details. Remember: The universe doesn't work for you.

Step 3: Make Peace with Potential Pains of Pivoting

Have you ever thought about making peace with the worst-case scenario of a situation BEFORE you switch gears?

For me, it's a common practice, because I've found that weighing the cons of a decision or goal prepares me to overcome any obstacles that may present themselves along my journey.

I did this before I went to South Korea. I read about the cons of living in a small village as opposed to a big city. I read about the cultural differences that many people found annoying. I read about the "horror" stories of bad co-teachers and entitled students.

Maybe this kind of research is not for every personality type, but I'm able to read these accounts while maintaining full awareness that everyone's experience is unique and other people's perception is their reality and theirs alone.

That said, I assessed these cons--or pain points--and asked myself how I would deal with this situation if I experienced the same scenario on my journey. I asked myself, "what's the worst that could happen?" For me, nothing was really a deal-breaker or something I felt like I couldn't handle. I decided to pursue the endeavor anyway, in spite of the cons. Moreover, I never gave much thought to those potential pain points after making the decision to move forward.

I expected the best yet visualized myself overcoming the worst. Visualization is powerful, and I recommend it wholeheartedly on this journey.

That said, I am fully aware that not everyone has the capacity to assess the worst-case scenario so objectively without experiencing extreme anxiety. It can be hard to wrap your mind around how you'd deal with a particular pain.

My advice to you is to ask yourself if the worst-case scenario of the pivot is worse than remaining in your current situation. Which of the two evils, if you had to choose, would you rather experience?

If your current situation is worse than "the worst that is likely to happen", it's definitely time to pivot!

The 7 Potential Pains of Pivoting

I want to help you make peace with the potential pains of pivoting (Daannnggg!! I impressed my damn self with that alliteration!).

Granting yourself permission to pivot is not all sunshine and rainbows, no matter how punchy the title is. Surely, going against the grain will bring its own set of struggles; but hey, what's life without a little strife?

In order to make peace with the potential pains, we need to know what they are, right? I pinpointed seven potential pains of which I think you should be aware (not afraid).

Potential Pain #1:

You have to say goodbye to what was once comfortable, familiar, predictable, and safe.

Listen, this is not fun. I don't know about you, but I enjoy being comfortable. The problem with comfort is that very little growth happens there. I've read countless memoirs and biographies of successful people and to be quite honest with you, not one journey sounded comfortable, safe, or predictable.

Potential Pain #2:

You don't receive praise or support from loved ones regarding your new decision, goal, or direction.

Quite honestly, you're going to intimidate people with your audacity to do shit on your own terms. As humans, we prefer to be praised and revered, not shamed and ridiculed, but on this journey, you have to make peace with the fact that some friends and family will not be along for the ride. AND THAT'S

OKAY. As you change your gotdamn mind, some will be left behind. This is not the U.S. Education system; you don't need to wait for them to catch up.

Potential Pain #3:

The pursuit is much harder than you ever anticipated.

Let's be real, sometimes we embark on journeys and we don't realize until we're waist deep that they are going to be hard AF. But you and I both know that anything worth having usually doesn't come easy, and just because a decision or goal is hard does not justify a pivot. Difficulty builds character. Pressure makes diamonds.

Potential Pain #4:

There are no immediate signs that you made the right choice.

Truth be told, there won't always be immediate signs that you've made the right decision. It may take a while for your tree to bear fruit. However, it serves no one for you to be impatient or operate from a mindset of instant gratification. You are not Aladdin. There is no wish-granting Genie. You must work hard, sow seeds, and wait the proper amount of time for your flowers to bloom.

Potential Pain #5:

Reality fails to meet your unrealistic expectations.

I guess we all set goals and have expectations of how said goals will ultimately manifest, but the truth is that while you have the power to manifest your deepest desires, the plan you put into place may not always go as you'd hoped, and you do not have the power to determine exactly how said desire will come to fruition. There is a reason why the Greats in personal growth and development say to get clear on the "what," take action, but don't get bogged down by the intricacies of the "how."

Potential Pain #6:

You may disappoint some people in your life who will be affected by your pivot.

I know what you're thinking, but this is different from the Potential Pain #2. This pain point is referring to those whose lifestyle will be affected in some way by your pivot. It's no secret that we live in a society that has touted this nonsense idea that we are to place others' needs, wants, and desires ahead of our own. A word like "selfish" has a negative connotation, because we are programmed to believe that doing what's best for ourselves is a "bad thing" if it leaves someone we love in a bind or less than comfortable situation.

I call bullshit. Sorry, not sorry. If you are making a healthy decision for yourself that leaves a grown-ass person in your life uncomfortable or in a less than fortunate situation, because they were dependent on you remaining in a less than healthy or desirable state, then to you, I say, carry on sis. Carry on! It is not--and should have never been--your job to remain unfulfilled for the sake of someone else's fulfillment.

Potential Pain #7:

You'll have to go toe to toe with your imposter: that little voice in your head who will constantly tell you that you can't do it.

Who wants to box with their imposter? Most of us would just rather not talk to her, if we're being honest. She's negative AF, always assuming the worst, and prefers that you marinate in misery instead of challenging yourself to do and be better. I know she's a pain in the ass. I feel you, but you'd better believe beyond a shadow of a doubt she'll be there every damn time you decide to grant yourself permission to pivot. She doesn't like change, challenges, or struggle... all of which you sign up for when you change your gotdamn mind.

So here we are. Seven potential pains of pivoting with which you must make peace before granting yourself permission to pivot. If they sound too painful, maybe you're not ready to pivot. I don't say that to be mean or condescending, I say that because, as Jay Shetty said,

"When the pain of remaining the same is GREATER than the pain of change, only then will you change."

And that's what's real, folks. It's that simple. For me, it's cathartic to make peace with potential pains before they arise. I feel like I have a leg up or something. Maybe that's not your thing... maybe you prefer to walk in blindly and deal with each pain as they arise, but I've found that visualizing how my best self would overcome such pain is highly therapeutic and rewarding and makes navigating through the struggles of the "how" so much more manageable. That's just me.

Step 4: Change Your Mind, Then Mind the Damn Change

Unless the criteria for a purposeful pivot has been met, respect the journey of the pivot and don't quit.

Why do I say this? It may be tempting to change your mind again and again and again, because ease never seems to show its face after a change has been made. After you choose to pivot, make your plan, and make peace with the worst-case scenario and all the potential pains of the pivot, you have to then take action. You have to stick with it-- no deviating from the plan unless the situation warrants it (and you can refer back to Part 2 to determine whether that's the case).

A great way to help you stick to the path is to visualize the process from start to finish. See yourself basking in the moment when it becomes clear that you made the right decision. Think and feel what that looks like. Journal it. Create a vision board. Get excited about the journey. Mind the change, because your pivot deserves a chance to prosper.

I want you to treat your decision to pivot as if it's a promise. Do you remember when you were younger, and you wanted to be 100% sure your friend was telling the truth or fully committed so you asked them to "pinky promise?" Well, channel that same energy when it comes to your pivots. These are literally promises you're making to yourself; they hold just as much weight as a promise to a friend or a family member. The promises you make to yourself deserve to be kept unless the situation meets the criteria discussed in part 2 for changing it. You have to be a woman of your word. If it were easy, you wouldn't have needed to go through this pivot process in the first place.

It's not going to be easy, but always remember that following through is how you get the most out of each and every pivot. You must COMMIT in every sense of the word.

Step 5: Evaluate & Elevate Your Environment

Once you've committed to your pivot, the natural thing to do is evaluate your current environment and assess what changes need to be made in order for your pivot to have the best chance at survival.

What do I mean, exactly?

Well, sometimes we make hard decisions to change, but we don't make sure our environment supports that change.

I can think of a prime example:

My friend made a conscious relationship pivot that entailed her going from in a relationship to single. She broke up with her boyfriend of 7 years. You can imagine after a 7-year relationship, a lot of other areas would be affected. He was living with her, they shared a car, they also had mutual friends, and they had a trip planned that was non-refundable.

Here's what she did:

She felt trapped and didn't want to kick him out, so she agreed to let him stay until he "got on his feet." The car was in her name and she paid the note, but she continued to let him use it and kept him on her insurance policy. She would unload their private business onto all of their mutual friends (none of whom were in healthy relationships of their own), who would in turn constantly add their "two-cents" and give bad advice. She even let him talk her into going on the trip with him, since it was already paid for.

She decided to pivot, but never optimized her environment to match the decision. It was no surprise when they found themselves in an on again, off again situation. It would have been a never-ending cycle had she not put her foot down, kicked him out, and severed all ties. Some decisions require much more than a "dip-your-toe-in-to-see-if-it's-warm" approach.

Part 4
Setting Yourself Up for Success in Pivoting

I am a STRATEGIST to my core (shout out to all my INTJs!). As a strategist, I'd be remiss if I didn't share with you my best strategies for pivoting like a pro.

Because the truth is, the most successful pivots are those backed by an action-packed plan of attack!

The Strategy Behind Changing Your Gotdamn Mind

There's a reason I started this book by talking about self-awareness. Without it, you'll find yourself either stagnant like Stacy, or worse, on an endless journey of meaningless pivots that won't lead you to your destiny. To avoid both scenarios, you get to know who you are, what drives you, how you show up for yourself and how you ultimately want to show up for others. One of my goals is to make sure you'll do the work in that area before committing to any major pivots. Assuming that you've done the work in getting to know yourself better, I can now share with you the strategies you'll want to implement as you decide to change your mind.

You remember the 10 main areas of pivoting, right?

1. Personal Pivots
2. Relationship Pivots
3. Professional Pivots
4. Educational Pivots
5. Spiritual Pivots
6. Lifestyle Pivots
7. Mental Pivots
8. Financial Pivots
9. Physical Pivots
10. Values-Based Pivots

Well, there's a way to pivot successfully in each of those areas.

Let me explain:

You'll start by crafting a new routine for your pivot so that your body, mind, and environment can adjust to the new normal. Change is not always easy, and you want to give yourself a fighting chance when it comes to "minding the damn change," like we discussed earlier. What better way to do that than to form a new habit or routine around the new change?

If you haven't already done so, you'll want to get your finances in order. This is a given if you're making a financial pivot, but many people don't realize that money holds them back from making relationship pivots, educational pivots, physical pivots and more. Money matters more than we'd like to admit.

Let's face it, if you're not pivoting from a toxic relationship because that toxic partner of yours pays half the rent, then we have a serious problem. That is why money management is so important. So, get those financials in order sis, whatever that means for your situation.

Next, you'll want to track and analyze the success of your pivots. And I don't mean try it out for a week and abort the mission when you don't see the results you were hoping for. You have to really lay the groundwork, give your mind, body, and spirit time to adjust, and pivot only when the situation warrants it. You can revisit the criteria for pivoting in Part 2.

Then, you'll want to assign yourself a "Pivot Partner," more commonly referred to as an accountability partner. Ideally, this will be someone who has successfully pivoted in the area you are pivoting in, someone who has your best interest at heart, and someone who will humbly and lovingly slap some sense into you when you start overreacting.

Take all of this a step further by creating a pivot-specific vision board where you'll showcase what that area of your life looks like at its best. Visualization is a powerful tool. You'll visualize everything being exactly as it should be without giving much thought to the "how."

3 Pro Tips for Pivoting

No matter how self-aware or strategic you are, you can still run the risks of making mistakes during the process. In my opinion, mistakes are just lessons learned the hard way. Oftentimes, we benefit from having made those mistakes, but my pain tolerance is MAD LOW, so I prefer to do things right the first time whenever possible.

I'll take a wild guess and say you'd like to make this process as painless as possible, too. If so, here are some pivot pro tips and friendly reminders to help you navigate the process with just a little finesse. Of course, I can't offer you a completely pain-free pivot process, and anyone who does guarantee such a thing is lying to you.

Tip #1: Curate your circle carefully.

And I do mean CAREFULLY. There's nothing worse than gearing up to pivot into your purpose, only to be shut down by the company you keep. It is your duty to guard your goals and protect your pivots against pessimistic people. You don't need to justify your decision or goals to people who will never understand you. In fact, I encourage you to be like my friend Richie.

Richie keeps a list of people in his wallet whose opinion of him really matters. Every time he starts to question himself or his decisions because of something negative someone around him said, he pulls out his list and reminds himself that if their name isn't on it, he doesn't trust their opinion of his decisions or goals, and what they think of him doesn't matter, because if it did, their name would be on that list.

Try coming up with your own list! My list is pretty short.

List of People Whose Opinions Matter:

- ✓ Me
- ✓ Myself
- ✓ I
- ✓ God

Yup, that's about it. Not everyone chooses to match my level of sass. Your list is yours. Put down whoever deserves a spot and remember that moving forward, if the person giving you their unsolicited commentary about your life choices is not on that list, you can do one of two things:

1. **The Petty Option:** Hit 'em with the ole "Bye Felicia!"

2. **The Mature Option:** Thank them for their time, comments, and concern, and continue on having a blessed day.

The way my attitude is set up, I'm more inclined to go with option one, but I'm a work in progress; the Lord ain't through with me yet. Are there people whose opinions I value and would consider when it comes to the smaller scale pivots? Sure. But do I allow those people's opinions of how I walk in my purpose to keep me from walking in my purpose? Absolutely not.

Tip #2: Seek advice only from those who've been where you're trying to go.

This tip is closely related to the first, but it goes a step further and addresses the kind of person from whom you should take advice (while the other deals with opinions and support). It's the classic example of taking fitness advice from someone who's fit.

For the sake of our example, let's take it even further and imagine you have two personal fitness trainers, one of whom has been slim her entire life due to genetics. Sure, she's toned, knowledgeable, and knows her way around a gym, but she's never known what it's like to be obese. On the other hand, you have a trainer who lost 100lbs. She struggled with her weight her entire life, and she was able to reach her goal weight naturally.

You're interested in losing weight because you're obese, much like the second trainer used to be. Her story captivates you and while you know both trainers are professionals, you feel trainer number two can empathize and relate to all the pains you're experiencing and can more than likely anticipate the pains ahead as you decide to begin your fitness journey. Whose advice do you think will get you to where you want to go the fastest?

This is just an example, and the truth is, we can learn from a lot of different people depending on the situation. This is not to say that those who haven't been where you've gone can't help you, it just means you have to take their advice with a grain of salt. It's like Queen Beyonce said, "If you don't jump to put jeans on, baby you don't feel my pain."

We all want a (S)hero we can relate to.

Tip #3: Identify the worst-case scenario and visualize yourself overcoming it.

I included this tip for those who can't help themselves. No matter how many times they read that it's counterproductive to always think about the worst-case scenario, you'll have those who literally can't help themselves. They try to think positive thoughts. They try to speak positive words and affirmations, but they still can't help but think "what ifs."

If you fall into this category, don't worry, I'm not judging you. Or at least, I'm not judging you without offering you some constructive feedback. There's a way even YOU can turn those negative thoughts into positive ones. All you have to do is think about what it would look and feel like for your BEST self to overcome the negative scenario that keeps swarming around in your head.

I did this once when I was being bullied in the 6th and 7th grade. This little boy tried to make my life a living hell, and all I would do is fantasize about kicking his ass one day. Listen, I was 12! The Lord was just getting started with me. I rolled my eyes when my pastor would read the passage about "turning the other cheek." All I could think about was how much longer the bullying would go on if I didn't stand up for myself. Then, I consulted with my grandma (she was definitely on my list) and she gave me her blessing, she basically told me (and I'm paraphrasing) that all I had to do was lose my mind on that boy one time!

#PERMISSIONTOWHOOPHISASSGRANTED

Thanks grandma! May her sweet soul rest in power. Just like in my visualization, I came out triumphant! I should have probably fantasized NOT getting suspended, but a one-day suspension as opposed to another year of misery, I'll take it. The thing is, I may have manifested that fight itself by fantasizing about it so much, but at the time it felt like that particular outcome was inevitable since all the other steps I took didn't work.

My advice will ALWAYS be to replace all negative thoughts with positive ones, but, if you truly feel like you can't, this tactic is the best advice I can give. Envision yourself victorious.

Pivot Reminders

Reminder #1: Some promises are meant to be broken.

In case you haven't noticed, that's the premise of this book. You may end up granting yourself permission to pivot, committing to a promise, and then finding yourself in a situation that warrants a change. There's absolutely nothing wrong with this. As Sarah Steckler from the Mindful Productivity Podcast said, "you need to embrace the fluidity of your desires and decisions."

This does not mean you can go around casually breaking promises to yourself, but it does mean you can feel unapologetic about abandoning an ambition that no longer serves your best interest. Use the pivot criteria, ask yourself the hard questions, and do what's best for your star player.

Reminder #2: The plan is just as important as the execution.

The strategist in me won't let you forget to plan the work and work the plan. Taking action is essential, and there's something to be said for taking blind action and jumping before you're ready, BUT having that plan to back up that action gives you a special kind of peace that I'm sure anyone, including the fly-by-the-seat-of-your pants gals, can appreciate.

Maybe you're not a natural planner, and that's okay. Get you someone on your team who is. I love having people around me whose strengths compliment my weaknesses; this is another reason why self-awareness is key.

Reminder #3: The mind needs time to adjust after a major pivot, and so does the world around you.

Listen, love, no one adapts to drastic change overnight. It's okay to give yourself time and grace throughout the pivot process. You're not expected to just wake up and jump into your new normal like nothing's changed. Allow yourself to feel whatever it is you need to feel. If it's a loss of some kind, allow yourself time to grieve that loss. If it's a change in scenery, allow yourself time to mourn the previous scene. It's okay to feel.

Things get harder when you bottle up your feelings or underestimate the toll the recent change can have on you. If you genuinely want to pivot like a pro, you'll face and make peace with anything or anyone you have to give up in order for your pivot to take place.

Reminder #4: The grass is not always greener on the other side.

I really don't want this to come out the wrong way, but I have to say it. Obviously, the whole point of pivoting is to formulate a better reality than the current one. Why pivot if we don't believe things will be better? Well, the truth is, pivoting may be the right thing to do, but that doesn't always mean the positive effects are guaranteed (especially not immediately).

Some pivots take longer than others to yield positive gains. You may know deep down that you are meant to study law, not education. That doesn't mean that changing your major to law is going to be a cakewalk. It will be hard. It will require your proverbial blood, sweat, and tears, but sticking with it and seeing it through is where the benefits reside. Nothing worth it ever comes easy.

Reminder #5: The devil is always working 24/7/365, no matter how perfectly planned your pivot may be

Again, I say this not to scare you, but to remind you to keep the faith, because you will be tested. We are constantly being tested. Can we walk the talk, practice what we preach, and show up in faith even when the going gets tough? I mentioned before the pains of pivoting and pivot pitfalls etc., but your mindset has to be prepped and primed for the unfathomable.

This is obviously easier said than done, but if you're a believer you have to develop unshakeable faith. You can start by reading the works of Florence Scovel Shinn and Napoleon Hill. These two personal development authors have completely changed my life and mindset and I think their works can do the same for you.

Part 5

Be Unbreakable in Your Pursuit

Remember Stagnant Stacy and Audacious Audrey? As you read this book, did you think about which of those two Avatars you want to choose moving forward?

In this game of life, we have choices. Sure, there are a lot of circumstances that are completely outside of our control, but we ALWAYS have control over how we respond to the challenges we face. I want to respond with the audacity and the tenacity of Audrey.

What about you?

I know it's easier said than done. That under-discussed, underrated, yet uber important aspect of life called self-awareness is where it begins. Once we have an understanding of how to cultivate self-awareness, we're off to the races.

Then, knowing what we know about who we are and how we want to show up in the world, we have to decide which aspect of our life warrants a pivot and why.

Once we've decided that a particular area of our life meets the qualifying criteria of a purposeful pivot, we must plan that pivot like a bona fide pro by following the rest of the Pivot Protocol.

As part of that process, we tap into the strongest and most courageous parts of ourselves to make peace with the pains of the pivot, understanding that choosing to remain stagnant instead would be far more painful than making the change.

Once we've made peace, it's time to cultivate self-discipline and create a strategy that would give us the best chances of pivoting profitably, productively, and purposefully. Not everyone's a strategist. I get that. That's why I've suggested you go through the [companion guide], complete the exercises, and ask and answer the hard questions; in short, DO THE WORK.

Because listen, the research is overwhelming. Studies like those of Brendon Burchard, and even some Harvard researchers, show that deathbed regrets are largely made up of what the person DIDN'T do, shots that person didn't take, and opportunities squandered. Rarely do people regret the risks they did take-- especially when they were mitigated risks.

If you're having trouble figuring out who you are and what you want out of life, revisit Part 1 (and travel! Nothing brings awareness faster than immersing yourself in different cultures).

If you're having trouble deciding whether or not it's time to pivot, revisit Parts 2 and 3, and ask yourself the hard questions outlined in the [companion guide]. Channel your analytical avatar.

If you're feeling uneasy, unmotivated, unsure, or unprepared, revisit Part 4 and the strategy session in your [companion guide].

Start here but commit to making the decisions that place you in the best position possible to win.

If you need more one-on-one help, and I'm still offering that kind of coaching at the time you're reading this, reach out to me. I am fiercely passionate about empowering others to profitably pivot into their purpose and their absolute best life.

I want to go on this journey with you.

Take Action NOW

If you want to get started right now, I suggest the [companion guide and the pivot planner]. You'll gain clarity first and from there you'll be able to plan a strategic pivot that you won't regret.

The Potential of a Purposeful Pivot

I know some of you are dying to see how a purposeful pivot can be powerful in real life, so I've decided to shine the light on a few people you may know whose pivots have led them to success beyond their wildest dreams.

Let's take Robin Rihanna Fenty, for example:

Rihanna began her career in 2005 at the age of 16, with Jay-Z under Def Jam Records. She went on to produce six albums with that record label and eight total in her career.

In 2014, she decided to pivot into the fashion industry, teaming up with Puma and launching her line of sneakers and slippers called Fenty x Puma.

In 2017, she decided to pivot into the beauty industry, and launched her iconic Fenty Beauty line where she set the new standard for inclusivity by launching over 40 different shades of foundation.

As if that wasn't ambitious enough, in 2018 she launched Savage x Fenty, an inclusive and sexy lingerie line that caters to women of all shapes and sizes.

Did I forget to mention that throughout her career she also dabbled in acting? She appeared in movies like *Battleship, Bring It On, Guava Island*, and *Ocean's 8*.

You see, this woman refused to be placed in a box. She wore whichever hat suited her in the season she was in. She even pivoted in the type of music she produced, because she allowed herself to evolve with each season of her life. When she wanted to act, she acted. When she wanted to sing, she sang. When she wanted to start her own line of shoes, she did just that. When she wanted to launch her own line of beauty products, she did that too.

Her relationship pivots were also front and center. She dated men like Chris Brown (and we all know why she had to pivot out of that relationship), Drake, Matt Kemp, and her most recent boyfriend Hasan Jameel. With each of these men, Rihanna had to grant herself permission to pivot when the relationship was no longer serving her best interest.

She is a classic example of an Audacious Audrey. I sincerely doubt she sought the approval of others; she did what was best for her. She granted herself permission to change her gotdamn mind, unapologetically.

Then we have Dwayne "The Rock" Johnson:

I don't give a lot of male examples, but his story is amazing, and I grew up obsessed with... ahem... I mean watching his career. Dwayne thought football would be his life, his calling, his career, but a few rough shoulder and back injuries, he laid that dream to rest.

Then he decided to follow in his father's and grandfather's footsteps and become a professional wrestler with WWF (currently known as WWE), winning a total of 11 titles and becoming one of the most iconic wrestlers of all time.

Throughout his wrestling career, The Rock was considered to be a "one-woman man." He married the beautiful and talented Dany Garcia back in 2001, and they remained married until 2007. It was less than a year later that he pivoted into the arms of Lauren Hashian, his current wife and the mother of two of his children. Some people are lucky and don't need to make a lot of pivots in this area of life, while some need more options before they find their one and only. The Rock was lucky enough to get it right the second time around.

In 2004, he left the wrestling world and entered the world of Hollywood entertainment. He has starred in countless movies like *The Rundown*, *The Mummy Returns*, and *The Scorpion King*, just to name a few. As soon as people started to box him into one category of movies, he rebelled.

He wanted to showcase his skills and began starring in a variety of movies like *The Game Plan*, *The Other Guys*, *The Fast & the Furious* franchise, *Moana*, and *Baywatch*. All of these movies required him to tap into a different style of acting.

And he didn't stop there... Dwayne has occasionally returned to the wrestling world for major events like Wrestle Mania and Royal Rumble, showing the world that he's still got it. He has refused to play by anyone's rules but his own, and now he's one of the highest paid actors in the country. He didn't need permission from anyone but himself to change his gotdamn mind and pursue his wildest dreams. We'll call him Audacious Andre!

I'd be remiss if I didn't tell you all about multi-passionate, multi-talented, disruptor and rebel Teyana Taylor:

Teyana is a singer, songwriter, rapper, actress, choreographer, director, model, and brand ambassador. If you're thinking, "DAMN! The list of what this woman doesn't do would be a shorter list," you'd be right. The most amazing part of this is that she didn't need anyone's permission to wear all of these hats. She is one of the most authentic, ambitious, unapologetic women I know.

You may have seen Teyana on the formerly popular MTV Series, *My Sweet 16*. That's where she made her debut to the world. In 2005, Teyana signed a record deal with Pharell and Star Trak Entertainment. Under that label, she released her debut album *From a Planet Called Harlem* with her hit single, "Google Me."

In 2010, Teyana pivoted into acting and was featured in movies like Stomp the Yard: *Homecoming, House of Glam*, and *Madea's Big Happy Family*. She gave herself permission to act while still pursuing her musical career.

In 2012, she granted herself permission to pivot from the Star Trak label to the GOOD Music label under Kanye West. Why? Because Star Trak Entertainment was no longer serving her best interest. She left because she was unable to tap into her full potential. With GOOD Music, she went on to release three albums: *VII, K.T.S.E.* and *The Album*.

Teyana achieved a lot of these accomplishments as a wife to Iman Shumpert, NBA player, and as a mother to Junie and Rue... but she was not without relationship pivots. Before getting married to Iman, Teyana was engaged to Brandon Jennings for roughly four years, but when he cheated, she pivoted.

She dated men like Soulja Boy, Colin Kaepernick, and ASAP Rocky, but none of them were able to steal her heart the way Iman has. She's happily married, because she never settled.

From singing, to acting, to directing, to being a brand ambassador and creative director for one of the biggest online fashion retail stores in the world, she's proven that you can have it all if you really want it badly enough. And all of that while being a wife and mother? The woman has hats for days!

I included Teyana because out of all three stories, hers gets me every time. When I was in elementary school in Monroeville, PA, we got a new student named Teyana (Yes, THE Teyana!). She lived right next door to me, and we became instant friends. We'd sit in the hallway and write songs and sing together and although it was extremely short lived because she had to move, I'll never forget that she was just like me: no silver spoon, a product of a single-parent home, and operating on pure ambition. She made it happen for herself, and every time I look at her and all that she's accomplished, I feel like I can do anything I set my mind to.

I want you to know that you can too. There are so many examples out there of what happens when you remain true to who you are, what you want, and the process to get it. In order to get there, though, you first have to make the decision to operate outside of whatever box people are trying to put you in.

Parting Words From Your Pivot Partner in Crime

S top waiting for someone to tell you what to do next. Stop seeking outside validation for the decisions you know damn well only you should make. Stop allowing what other people "may" think to keep you from living your most authentic life.

As I write this book in 2020, I can't help but think of one thing: the finite time we have on this Earth. I think about that dash between our birth and our death. With so many premature deaths happening this year due to the COVID-19 pandemic, all I can think is, "What the hell am I going to do with my dash?"

I'll tell you this much: I'm not going to waste it. I'm going to do every damn thing I want to do because this is the only life I get, and I don't want to disrespect my dash by allowing someone else (or society in general) tell me how to live it.

Please understand this: the longer we wait to be who God has called us to be, the longer good people will suffer. I need you to know that and feel that on a visceral level. Let it convict you. Go out there and live your purpose. Do it unapologetically. When something or someone no longer serves your best interest, grant yourself permission to pivot. Period.

Acknowledgments:

To my husband Ilya: Thank you for your undying support throughout this process. I know it couldn't have been easy fending for yourself on days I was too busy to cook.

To my family: Thank you all for supporting every single project I do, even if you're not my target audience. That's love right there.

To my amazing editor, friend, and content creation analyst Payton: Thank you for dealing with my shenanigans, pushing me to finish, and making me look and sound so good.

To my sister-friend Taneeka: Thank you for being a rock during my hardest pivot. Without you, I may not have reached a point where I can live to tell about these pivots.

To my amazing beta readers Edem Adzaho, Alycia Austin, Sally Gachunji, Michaela Paluck, Jasmine Hubbard, and Litany Lineberry: You ladies are the real MVPs, and I can't thank you enough.

To my GLOW Gals: Thank you for being the best support system, sisters, teachers, and confidantes a girl could ever hope for. Love you ladies.

To my launch team: I love how you guys show up and show out for me and for this book. It means so much to me.

GET THE PIVOT PLAYBOOK!

To get the best experience with this book, I've found readers who invest in **The Pivot Playbook** are able to implement faster and take the next steps needed to make a purposeful, profitable pivot.

You can get a copy by visiting:

www.mypivotplaybook.com

About Kierra

Kierra Asunauskas, Productivity Coach, Lifestyle Design Strategist, and Founder of Miss Unconventional, went from being rock bottom broke, unemployed, and lost to being a purpose-driven entrepreneur. The plethora of pivots that make up her journey can best be described as "unconventional". Today, Kierra is walking in her purpose teaching ambitious entrepreneurs how to take control of their time, set intentional goals, and pivot into their purpose.

Kierra is known for geeking out over vision boarding, travel, non-fiction books, planners, productivity, personal finances, and pasta! The girl loves pasta. Every book she writes aims to empower womxn to stop playing small, design a life that is in alignment with their personality, purpose and passions, and be unapologetically authentic!

Can You Help Me?

We all know that one person who may need a little extra push in granting herself permission to pivot. It would mean the world to me if you could buy a copy of this book for that special someone.

In addition, an honest Amazon review is one of the best ways you can support me. I rely on your feedback and I value your opinion.

Please head over to Amazon or wherever you purchased this book to leave an honest review.

I am eternally grateful,

Kierra Asnuaskas

www.ingramcontent.com/pod-product-compliance
Lightning Source LLC
Chambersburg PA
CBHW072043040426
42447CB00012BB/2988